self
limiting
Beliefs

PHil HAnseh

Hi

my name's Phil and I'm an artist. Wow, I gotta say it feels nice to say "I'm an artist" because there was a time in my life when that dream was gone. This is because I developed permanent nerve damage in my drawing arm and became an art school dropout. After many years away from art I eventually wrapped my mind around what was stopping me from pursuing art. Not just my shaky hand, but something much more emotional was in my way. This realization has led me down an unexpected path in life where the obstacles thrown my way are much more malleable than they originally seemed. Heck, some obstacles even become a good thing and become part of who I am. The information that led to this realization is what I'd like to share with you here. I hope that you'll dig in with curiosity and openness. The ideas may be quick and understandable or you may want to sit with them for a while. But either way I hope it can do for you what it has done for me. Honestly, not trying to be dramatic here, the idea changed my life.

A note
before getting
started

I would like
to give you a quick note
about the structure of this booklet. There are two main
portions. The first is the big idea with stories and
context. The second portion digs into deliberate steps
you can take to work through your challenge.

The reason I want to mention the layout is because you
might get everything you need from the first portion. Or
you may want to continue onward. Whichever way you
venture in, do what is best for you.

Another note i'd like you to keep in mind is the goal of
this booklet can take many forms : You might be
working on a physical task and need to shake things up.
You may be thinking about the emotional side of your
task, or you just desire to explore an idea and keep the
goal vague. You can approach this very seriously or
incredibly playful. There isn't one way to read through
this so keep what you need and ignore what doesn't
apply.

My last note is to not rush through this. Simply
recognizing and absorbing the main point is something
that I've been working on for years. I'm not kidding.

Cool, alright, let's do this. :)

\\!/

Contents

Part 1

Part 2

Part 1

Self Limiting Beliefs
vs
Limitations

We all are familiar with what a challenge is. I never really gave it much thought in my life because it seemed so straight forward. You know, a challenge, something to test your abilities, to make you better at whatever it is your doing. This turned out the opposite for me, I was confronted with a challenge in my life and I ran the other way. I quit pursuing and even making art altogether. When my hand began to shake and pain ensued, I thought I was done with art completely. Time to throw in the towel and start a new career I thought (and I did!). I had no idea how ridiculous this would sound in hindsight.

There's a chance you've heard my story. You can watch the TED Talk here (https://bit.ly/3iJ6TWe) if you desire. In a nutshell, it's a story about this real-life medical dilemma I faced that compromised the pursuit of my great love— making art—and describes how I overcame the crisis. My story is personal, but after speaking about it with audiences around the world, I realized it's also universal, since it's ultimately about overcoming challenges as a human being. During my unconventional career as a multimedia artist, I've found many techniques to support people in overcoming challenges, but the one I want to share in these pages is the most potent. It's a pathway to transformation I reverse-engineered after the difficult experience I had, and also after analyzing over 3,000 stories from people willing to share a part of their lives with me. One of those people is named Sarah, and I'll use her story to illustrate two important concepts I'd like you to know about. Those concepts are the underlying components in a challenge:

(1) Limitations
(2) Self-limiting beliefs (a.k.a SLBs)

These two concepts matter because they're surprisingly power-ful drivers behind many of our choices and behaviors. The relationship between them isn't discussed enough. When Limitations and Self-Limiting Beliefs are on good terms, they're like a programming language that makes software run. Their codes write orders that are being carried out, but the orders are behind the scenes, largely concealed and automatic.

This means that if we don't get clear about these ghosts in the machine, they can partly determine our fate.

It may sound dramatic, but it's true. You'll see.

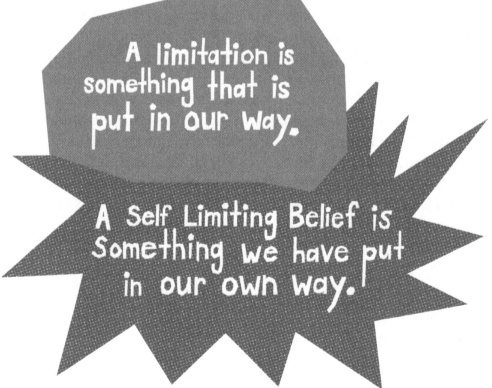

A limitation is something that is put in our way.

A Self Limiting Belief is Something we have put in our own way.

Limitations

Let's define the first concept: Limitations. Most people are familiar with the idea of a limitation and have experienced one or more. Limitations are real-world obstacles we face in pursuit of an ambition or goal. They have two defining characteristics:

(1) Limitations almost always represent a physical reality that's shared.
(2) Limitations do not change with hindsight.

Classic limitations to pursuing a project are—you guessed it—time and money. But as you might imagine, there are infinitely more. Limitations usually have a more clear solution then Self-Limiting Beliefs because they are easier to pinpoint and define. In the case of my personal story, my limitation was having permanent nerve damage that gave me a shaky hand, making art creation feel impossible. This lamentable physical state I was in checked the boxes of Limitations: The existence of nerve damage was agreed on no matter who was looking at it, and the condition didn't change with hindsight. There was a tough period in my life because I believed this Limitation would take me out of the art game forever. It didn't, because Limitations, alone, don't have that power per se, but I didn't know that at the time. Nor did I know that Limitations only generate power by latching themselves onto the second concept I want you to know: Self-Limiting Beliefs, or "SLBs."

A Limitation allows for possibility

Whereas

A Self limiting Belief blocks all paths and does not leave room for possibility

Self Limiting Beliefs (SLB's)

Self-Limiting Beliefs are the real powerhouse behind our blocks. Like Limitations, Self-Limiting Beliefs obstruct forward progress or movement, but they have distinct traits and qualities, for example:

(1) Self-Limiting Beliefs are invisible. They are not real-world and tangible.

(2) Because Self-Limiting Beliefs are invisible, they tend to stick around without us knowing it.

(3) SLBs find representation in our beliefs, attitudes, and per spectives and this gives them momentum.

(4) Self-Limiting Beliefs can reveal themselves differently in different environments. They can and do change with hindsight and effort.

(5) Self-Limiting Beliefs are derived from and perpetuated by our families, friends, and the culture-at-large, and they're formed after we experience, witness, or imagine an event.

(6) SLBs often lead to feelings of being dissatisfied or stuck and can cause quite a bit of mysterious friction in relationships.

Self Limiting Beliefs are sometimes trickier to identify than Limitations because we often think our beliefs ARE real limitations! Fun stuff. Take me for example, I believed that an artist can't have a shaky hand because of what society and life experiences had taught me. I've heard stories and had family-friends who have developed tremors later in life and it curtailed their art. This belief was a reasonable conclusion based on what I experienced but as you well know an artist CAN have a shaky hand. Their art will just look a little different.

Quick Sidenote - If you don't like me using the word belief, let's quickly break down myt word choice. A belief can be rephrased as a conviction, perspective, opinion etc. All you have to do is have coffee with a human and you'll realize that we have all manner of beliefs—in fact, entire belief systems—that help us form opinions, make decisions and move through the world. Beliefs and belief systems are required to live life. They only become self-limiting when they prevent us from getting to where we need to go. When that happens, SLBs are like gremlins after midnight. If we don't find them and corral them skillfully, they become reckless and disruptive, causing us unnecessary troubles.

Like Limitations, SLBs come in infinite shapes and forms, so the pathway I'll get to in a bit will be evergreen. You'll be able to use it over and over to work with almost any challenge you'd like rethought and hopefully undone.

At this moment I'd like to introduce you to Sarah. She called into the studio and shared her story with me while I was collecting these stories for a project about limitations, and it will help illuminate these concepts, so let's step into her world.

Sarah's Story

Sarah was one of the 3,000 people I connected with to learn more about Limitations and SLBs. She was diagnosed with an impulse-control disorder called trichotillomania in her adolescent years and this was decidedly her Limitation. Trichotillomania is a disorder that causes people to pull out their own hair, so she had large bald patches on her head. It affects women about ten times more than men and many of those folks, like Sarah, experience public shaming around this condition. They endure a lot of embarrassment. Sarah shared with me what it was like to live with trichotillomania, a very real Limitation. This Limitation fit the two criteria perfectly: It represented a physical reality that other people concurred with, and hindsight wouldn't have changed its existence.

Living with this Limitation, Sarah described feeling stifled all the time. Because of the baldness her condition caused, she wore wigs and couldn't do basic teenage-girl activities.

She couldn't go to sleepovers and have her hair braided. She never went swimming. She didn't ride rollercoasters. She didn't let her boyfriend touch her hair.

And the list goes on...

Sarah didn't even roll car windows down for fear of her wig blowing off. She described her life as "doors closing all around," and no matter how difficult it got, she could not find freedom living with this Limitation. On her personal path to change, she would become clear about the real force behind the Limitation's power.

I mentioned Sarah was an adolescent girl, which means she's aware of one expectation young girls forever face: long, beautiful hair. Sarah struggled with the prevailing social demand—a belief she unconsciously absorbed—not only that a girl HAS hair, but that the hair "is thick and luscious and lovely." Shaving her head and being bald was one possible solution, but it required blowing past the idea that a real girl has gorgeous locks. "Man," Sarah said, "I can't tell you how many times I have been tormented by that expectation."

As we chatted, Sarah told me she was considering the idea of embracing her Limitation by getting rid of the wigs she wore and shaving her head. The idea of doing this scared her, of course, but she wanted to stop hiding and missing out. She said she was wearing "a mask" for everyone else but it was starting to have too high of a price in her life.

"I was
pulling off a
mask and I
wasn't sure if
I liked
what I saw
underneath it
because

I was
wearing the
mask for
everyone else,
but I didnt
realize that
I had been
wearing it
myself as
well "

She recognized that the real culprit, the invisible influencer, was the Self- Limiting Belief attached to it. Her belief that a young woman should have hair that "is thick and luscious and lovely." Sarah longed to discard her wig immediately after graduation. She pondered it...sat with it...wrestled with it...

...and finally did it. Sarah shaved her head. Bald. And threw away her wigs.

At first, she said, she wasn't sure if she liked what she saw, but she was determined to forgive herself for a condition she couldn't control. **She was tired of calling something "freedom" that was actually holding her back.** Once Sarah banished her wig, almost overnight her world got better. "All around me doors have just blown open," she said, "I can do whatever I want! And it feels so good. It feels so good."

I wish everyone could know the freedom Sarah gave herself. Her joy and relief were palpable. If you watch the video (the video for the artwork Refraction on my website), you'll see she looks like a different girl, one shining from the inside. It's important to pause and see that Sarah had within herself something that all of us do: the ability to unlearn a self-imposed story. She had uncovered her SLB lurking in the shadows of her mind and challenged herself to let it go. Because she did, her Limitation—one that seemed insurmountable for so long—lost all of its power.

Hopefully through this story you're beginning to understand how potent the combined forces of Limitations and Self Limiting Beliefs are, and how much they can change the course of your life. Sarah's physical Limitation was real. She did have challenges with impulse control that resulted in persistent hair loss. But what she believed about that reality was the bigger problem. As she identified and worked with her Limitation and its attached SLB, she blew open the doors of her perception and found a new reality.

I may be making it sound easy to blast through Limitations and Self-Limiting Beliefs, and sometimes it is. But more often than not, these phenomena are all tangled up, and that's when the going can get tough. But when we are able to recognize our beliefs for what they are, malleable, we can begin to discover, reshape and build our own definitions of beauty, success, age, disability, and so much more!

How Beliefs Form

As I was digging further into beliefs I noticed that they can change with age or they can stay steady forever. Beliefs can be adopted from people around us and our beliefs can be adopted by others. We can actively work at forming a belief or a belief can take root in our brains without our awareness. But still the question lingered with me, how do beliefs form?

To see how beliefs develop we need to step waaaaay back because it usually doesn't happen in a day (unless it's traumatic). The formation process is straightforward and can be summarized like this.

1. We have an experience.
2. We replay it and make judgments about it.
3. We draw conclusions and form opinions.
4. Then we take action.

Then a funny thing happens, we loop. The loop happens the next time we run into a similar experience, we instantly project our past opinions and judgements onto this new experience. For example, I still remember the first, second, and third time I spoke on stage. I was always sweaty, went blank, and felt sick. This experience kept happening again and again. It made me think to myself, "Well, clearly I'm bad at this. Don't think I want to do that again!". And while not all beliefs are bad, I think you can see how we can loop ourselves into Self-Limiting Beliefs.

One important thing to reiterate before we dig in is that not all beliefs are limiting. In fact, most of our beliefs and judgements about the world are either good or go unnoticed because they don't cause problems. It's only when a belief causes friction or prevents us from moving ahead that it becomes limiting. Again, my belief that an artist can't have a shaky hand wasn't a problem until I developed a tremor. Vigilance to our ever changing existence in this world is massively important.

As I spent more time researching the formation of beliefs I came across work by Chris Argyris who was an organizational psychologist. His work expands on what I've already laid out. By analyzing our thoughts and actions against this ladder we can begin to break down why we react to certain things the way we do. Why others may react differently to the same experience and what we can do to stop the looping process. I'd like to suggest coming back to this a few times as there is always more to be personally discovered.

(diagram starts from the bottom - just like a ladder)

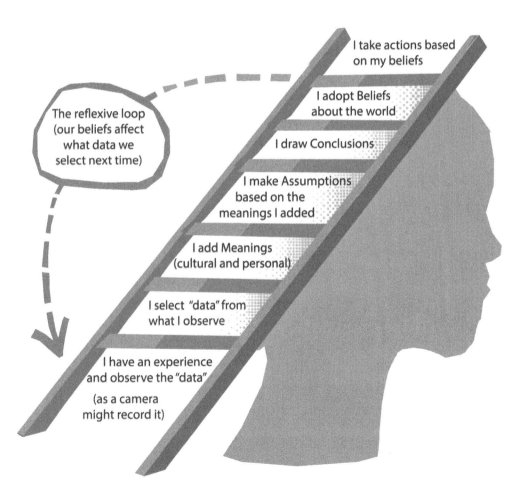

I take actions based on my beliefs

I adopt Beliefs about the world

The reflexive loop (our beliefs affect what data we select next time)

I draw Conclusions

I make Assumptions based on the meanings I added

I add Meanings (cultural and personal)

I select "data" from what I observe

I have an experience and observe the "data"

(as a camera might record it)

Let me tell you a story about Susan to illustrate how the ladder can play out.

Susan is pretty darn good at singing but is nervous to sing in front of others. She tries out for the high school musical and is scared and excited when she gets a role with a solo. She participates in the rehearsals but during the first performance she hears people snickering during her solo. Here's how the ladder plays out for Susan. (Starting again at the bottom)

(7) I rehearse for everything.
(Even things that seem simple)

(6) I must practice to be good at something

(5) I should have practiced more.

(4) Maybe I'm slightly off key. That is the only reasonable explanation for their laughter.

(3) They must be laughing at my singing

(2) I don't see anything happening that is funny

(1) I am singing and people are laughing.

Susan decides to rehearse and rehearse all week and at the next weekend's performance, Susan performs her solo and no one laughed. This confirms her belief that she needed to practice. Susan takes this embarrassing experience and lesson learned into other aspects of life and always puts in more practice time than others. Susan subconciously looks for reasons to practice which will confirm her belief, creating a reflexive loop (shown on previous page diagram). It serves her well. But, the thing that Susan never knew is that during her first solo her friend Rebecca, *always the goofball*, was making funny faces behind her. Susan developed a belief based on inaccurate data.

This experience Susan had is completely natural and normal. We do the same thing all the time. Whether intentionally or unintentionally we want to prove our gut feelings as correct. We look at our experiences to validate our beliefs.

Sometimes beliefs can serve us well but I think we can easily see how Susan could have decided not to try out for next year's play. One experience without proper analysis can become a snowball or even a self fulfilling prophecy.

Gaining awareness of our Limitations and our Self-Limiting Beliefs is a powerful exercise. As you digest these two concepts, give them plenty of time, don't rush it. On the following pages I give some ideas and recommendations of how to observe beliefs in others and some activities to begin analyzing yourself. Check those out and then decide if you want to venture in to Part 2.

Part 2 is where you will do the real heavy lifting and hopefully create some cracks to shed light on to the challenges you face.

~ Observation ~

⌣ Observe others and try to recognize their beliefs. Not their Self-Limiting Beliefs but just regular beliefs. (PLEASE don't point out the beliefs you observe but simply learn to recognize them). This is an important step in being able to reflect on ourselves. This is an activity you could do for a day or two or for a month.

⌣ Observe others and try to spot the confirmation loops they are making. If someone jumps to a conclusion that doesn't make sense to you, try to determine if they are bringing past experiences into the current experience. What sort of beliefs might be tied to this current experience?

⌣ Observe others and try to put yourself in their shoes. Try to empathize with their situation. For example, if someone is struggling with poor eyesight and is frustrated, squint your eyes so things are blurry and try to imagine how it would change your experience in the world.

Once you have done the activities above, repeat them but this time try to look for self limiting beliefs.

~ Reflection ~

━ Think about any beliefs that you have. Write them down and hold them in your head for a while. The beliefs don't have to be self limiting. This is just a moment to think about the beliefs that we have about our lives and the world. As you think about them, also ponder if any actions are tied to your beliefs.

━ Start to think about how your beliefs have affected the past. These could be the same beliefs as above or entirely new ones. What good things have come from your beliefs? Are there troubling things that have come from your beliefs? Take a moment to think and/or write your thoughts.

━ Is there a belief that causes friction when working towards a goal or desire in life? Try to pinpoint where/when that belief causes the most friction. The last reflections to leave you with are a few big questions. I recommend coming back to them from time to time.

━ When you isolate a belief, are you able to determine where it comes from? (culture, personal experience, parents, peers, etc) I find this very difficult to do but it can also be eye opening.

━ Why do you believe what you believe? Do you believe because it's true, due to social pressures, or you're not sure why but you've always believed it! Do you believe that this belief is true for everyone (perhaps if they were in your shoes?)

Part 2

Pathway to Transformation

Part 2
Overview

1   Identify the goal

2   Identify the Limitations

3   Identify the Self Limiting Beliefs

4   Generate Questions

5   Creative possibility

6   Taking action

1 Identify the Goal

All active pursuits involve a goal, an intention, and/or an aspiration. When you start the pathway to transformation for the first time, your goal might be something simple, like losing weight, getting better at public speaking, finding time for your creative passion, or downsizing your amount of belongings. Whatever it is, for our purposes, goal-identification doesn't need to take too much of your energy. The bulk of the work lies in steps 2 – 5. For this step, just consider and capture a goal you're currently sitting with. If you've printed this, you can write or draw that goal in the space provided or just write it on a piece of paper. I've included an example goal of "reducing stress" that we'll use throughout Part 2.

My goal is

_____

_____

_____

_____

_____

_____

_____

Phils example goal :   Reduce stress

2 Identify the Limitations

Identify the Limitations surrounding your goal.

Once you've identified a goal, the next step along this path is to identify what you believe are the tangible obstacles toward that goal. We're working to discover what you are experiencing to be Limitations to your destination. Maybe a Limitation is the fact that you work two jobs. Maybe a Limitation is that you don't have a reliable car, or your kid is suddenly home from school for weeks on end. Whatever your Limitations may be, lay them all out in this stage. You'll see from the visual below that Limitations can have many categories—material, financial, social and so forth, but remember : Limitations almost always represent a physical reality, one others can also see, and their existence does not change with hindsight. The exercise here is to make your Limitations explicit, so empty onto the page those real-world blocks you haven't yet found a way past.

For those of you who learn from sharing out loud, take this opportunity to confide in a friend or colleague about what's currently in the way. Often, externalizing our ideas about a situation helps us hear ourselves think. Whether you need to work solo or in tandem, do your best to pour out the truth about physical or tangible blocks related to the goal you chose.

To support your understanding of this part of the process, I wrote out some of the limitations I face on my way to "reducing stress". Utilize the blank space on the next page and start populating it. Lastly, please note that some categories may not fit perfectly with what you're up against, that's expected.

Sample : Limitations I find while trying to reduce stress.	
Material	The demands of being available 12+ hours a day to work is too much. But it's hard to only work set hours.
Financial	As an artist I find work to be unpredictable and this makes me a bit anxious.
Physical/ Medical	I'm not the fastest at tasks. I tend to need to rework things.
Time/ Life	Time is very tough because I get stressed not having time for my art because I need to work but I need to work in order to have money to make free time to create art
Social/ Political	I often feel societal pressure to ignore my stress and just work through it.

Write down any limitations that come to mind surrounding your goal.
(feel free to create your own categories)

Material	
Financial	
Physical/ Medical	
Time/ Life	
Social/ Political	

*Use this side if you need
more room or different categories

3 Identify the Self Limiting Beliefs

Identify the Self-Limiting Beliefs surrounding your goal.

This step requires a little heavier lifting—and a little more emotional honesty—since it's the stage where we start to discover our often-shadowy Self-Limiting Beliefs. Remember: SLBs are invisible. These fears, concerns, and ideas about a project don't represent a physical reality that anyone outside of us could point to. But you know by now that SLBs are often more—much more—influential than Limitations. They wrap transparent layers of 'no,' 'can't,' 'shouldn't,' and 'don't' around the momentum we're trying to build. SLBs pile onto that natural urge to take action, causing more and more friction until they grind our efforts or intentions to a halt. Now is your chance to write down all of those things that you believe about your limitations in the space to the right. It might take a few minutes to find the rhythm of distinguishing between a belief and a limitation, totally normal. And if they get a little mixed up it doesn't matter much. Just be as honest and self reflective as possible and write down your thoughts.

What do you believe about your limitations?
(Write it here, or on your own paper)

Sample: What I believe about reducing stress in my life.

- Stress is bad
- I have to get my work done
- Clutter makes me stressed
- I believe a big financial cushion is important
- I can't say "No" to work
- I'm not the sharpest tool in the shed
- I can't predict when things become too hectic and induce an angry stress reaction.

4 Generate Questions

Generate creative questions to rethink your beliefs.

Because they're subtle operators, private dancers, gremlins in the cogs, SLBs can be sticky, like gum on the bottom of your shoe. It helps when we shake, rattle, and roll them around not only to get curious about their existence, but also to get free of their influence. This process will be different for all of us but this step is sure to help this process get cranking. What we are aiming to do is come up with creative questions. You might be asking, what are creative questions? They are questions that might seem initially odd, or questions not worth asking, or questions that seem kind of "dumb". But if we take creative questions seriously we have real potential to rethink those beliefs. So take one of your belief statements on the previous page and put it in the center of the illustration to the right. Then begin to ask yourself those questions about the belief. Probe deep and look for answers that aren't on the surface, look for answers that seem impractical, look for answers that create more questions. As you dig in please note that the questions may need to be adapted slightly to whatever belief you plug in.

You might want to jump to the following page and see how I ran one of my beliefs about reducing stress through this process. To follow along with my process, start at the center and work your way out.

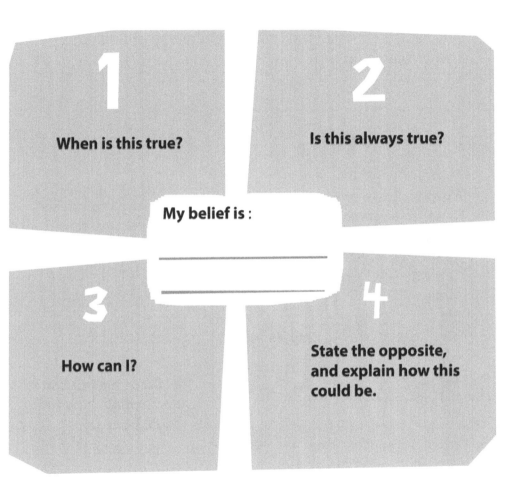

1

When is this true?

2

Is this always true?

My belief is :

_____

_____

3

How can I?

4

State the opposite, and explain how this could be.

37

Phil's Example #1

My goal is to reduce stress and one of the beliefs I identified is that, "Clutter makes me stressed." So I put that belief at the center of the chart and began to ponder. This is what I came up with.

1. When is this true?

Mostly at work, having the pressure to present myself in a certain way makes me worry about messes more. Rarely at home do I feel the same.

2. Is this always true?

Not always. Thinking about it: when I'm under more stress at work I get more stressed by the clutter around. So am I really stressed by the clutter?

My belief is:

clutter makes me stressed

3. How can I?

- How can I reduce clutter?
- How can I be less stressed by clutter?
- How can I reduce the things that make up clutter?
- How can I create a clutter free area at work?
- How can I relieve stress caused by clutter?

4. State the opposite, and explain how this could be true.

Clutter makes me calm. Oy! I guess sometimes it makes me more creative. And to a degree I save time not putting everything away perfectly. I can take my stress out on clutter and not hurt its feelings. Also owning things I can use for work brings me happiness.

Phil's Reflection

In the "**When is this true?**" category it made me realize when and where my belief that clutter makes me stressed is coming from. "clutter makes me stressed" is a blanket belief I jumped to when in fact I can hone it down to "clutter at work makes me stressed". I think getting more specific about my belief will help me out moving forward through the chart, and finding an action to reduce my stress.

In the "**Is this always true?**" section I think I refined my belief even further. It is more clear to me that clutter is more stressful when I am feeling overwhelmed or under more stress while at work. I could even restate my belief as "clutter at work adds to my stress level." Way more specific! This gives me something to think about when dealing with the clutter. Perhaps I can focus on cleaning up and preparing space before a major project or deadline?

In the "**How can I?**" category I was surprised how many questions I was able to give myself for practical steps I can take. This process got me wondering if I can simply reduce the things I own. I'll need to double check what I really need. I'm also trying to tell myself that clutter is okay in certain situations and places. Perhaps a small clutter free space to escape to when feeling stressed is all I need. I have a few possibilities to try out!

Emotional Impact:
I can definitely say that I don't feel quite as strongly about clutter making me stressed. I see there are some nuances to the concern and probably some practical things I can do. I'm feeling a little less stressed about the idea of clutter!

Phil's Example #2

1. When is this true?

When I'm neck deep in a project. I don't know I'm stressed until I react and communicate in a frustrated way to someone else.

2. Is this always true?

Not always. When I procrastinate on deadlines it happens more. Also when I am overly ambitous with what I can get done in a day.

My belief is:
I can't predict when my work load becomes too much.

3. How can I?

- How can I predict when my work load is too much?
- How can I be more aware of my own stress level?

4. State the opposite, and explain how this could be true.

I can predict when my work load becomes too much.
If I actually write down a list of all the things I need to get done in a day. Step back and give myself time to pause for a moment of reflection about what I need to get done. I think I'll be more realistic in what I can get done.
Also if I had clear signs of when I am stressed I could recognize it easier and take action to reduce work load and stress.

Phil's Reflection

I think we can see that my belief of "not being able to predict when my workload becomes too much" is tied up with many things. It was helpful to question where this belief comes from. Was it procrastination? Or being overly ambitious? Both? Those were good things to think about. It is obvious in hindsight that my daily ambition mixed with procrastination can lead to me overloading myself, and then making the conclusion that "I can't predict when my work load becomes too much."

If I have a lot to do, which is inevitable sometimes, I should probably fit in decompression time to my day.

Your Chart #1

No rush! Move slow, take your time. Go back and forth between the steps if you need to. What we are looking for here is discomfort and moments of pause.

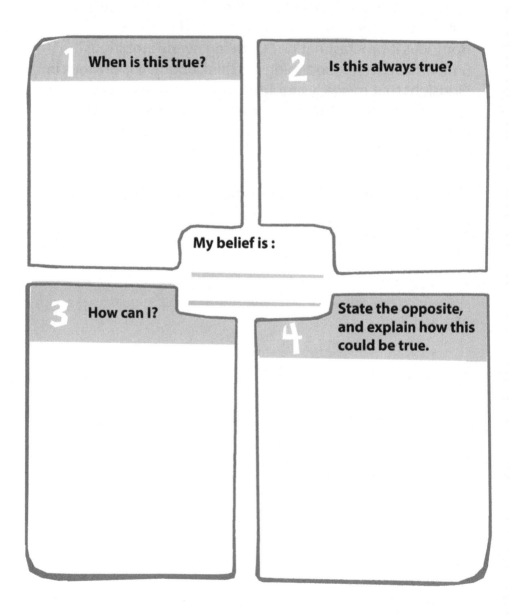

1 When is this true?

2 Is this always true?

My belief is :

3 How can I?

4 State the opposite, and explain how this could be true.

Reflection

**There is room to write on the next couple pages.
If you need some starter questions for your reflection,
give these a look.**

- Which question created the strongest reaction for you? Why?

- Can you perhaps start to see when/where the belief is the strongest?

- Did you think of a possible way forward? Sometimes a simple belief gets more complicated when you start to be specific about it.

- Which question would you like to think more about? Why?

- What voice are you noticing within yourself and in the chart? A happy tone, curious, sad, stubborn, annoyed, open minded, closed minded, etc.?

- Do you feel more open and ambiguous or are you feeling more frustrated? If you're feeling conflicted or confused, I believe that's a great place to be because it means our mind is trying to figure things out.

- If you're feeling overly frustrated, come back to this part again in a few days. It is a good place to be because, again, it means you may be working through something challenging but, it may be a sign that some time to ruminate is needed.

43

Your Chart #2

Here's another one. If you want more, you can print this page over and over or simply draw it out.

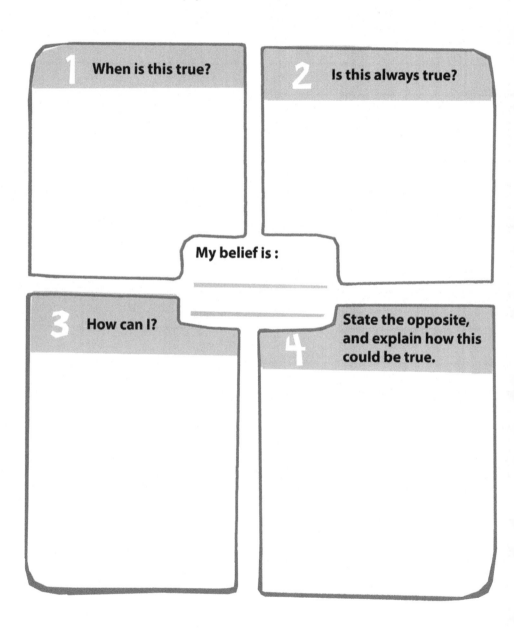

1 When is this true?

2 Is this always true?

My belief is :

_____

3 How can I?

4 State the opposite, and explain how this could be true.

Reflection

Refer back to pg 43 if you like to use the question prompts again.

I honestly believe that questioning our beliefs is the hardest thing we can do as people because it often questions our underlying values. Our values are often the most deeply embedded beliefs we have, we share them across family, across culture, and questioning them will often cause discomfort with our root selves. But this process is also incredibly important because our beliefs have so much impact on our lives.

So, "Woopa!" to you for taking these steps and beginning to dig deep. Depending on what you're contemplating you may already have some ideas of the next steps to take, are feeling more content, or you may have just cracked open a can of worms. Either way, enjoy the process of discovering an alternative, and hopefully more satisfied, you.

Through your thoughtful engagement with this process I'm sure you've seen what you're mind is capable of, and areas that need work or are holding you back. There is no question that this activity is truly a mental workout. The more you bend and flex what you think and believe the more resilient and adaptable you'll become. These traits can be very helpful in acheiving goals or perhaps brightening up a rough patch in life. They can also open more areas of life to explore. And who doesn't want that!

5 Creative possibility

Get creative with the Limitation and the Goal.

Rethink the Limitations

Now what we are going to do is take our limitations from step 2 and plug them into the same questions in step 4. Be prepared because it might be more challenging this time. The questions might not seem to fit but try your best to bend your mind around the question. Something really interesting might develop.

It's good to be aware that in this process you'll quite likely find a SLB and a Limitation tied together. Note it and carry on. By asking creative questions about our limitations we are trying to make sure our limitation is what we think it is and look for flexibility. Almost every time I do this process I find one of my limitations is tied together with a belief and I have to think and stare at the wall for a bit! :)

Rethink the Goal

Sometimes in this process it's helpful to put ourselves back at the beginning for a minute and rephrase our goal. If possible, get more specific in defining the goal. This will allow us to get more granular and maybe find more interesting answers to our creative questions.

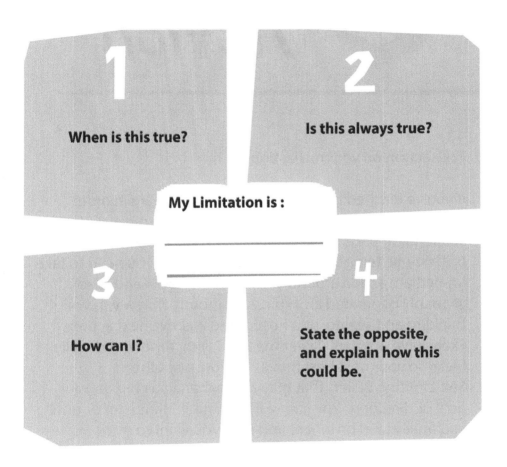

1

When is this true?

2

Is this always true?

My Limitation is :

_____

_____

3

How can I?

4

State the opposite, and explain how this could be.

51

6 Taking Action

Take action on your realizations.

If you've reached this stage, congratulations are in order because it means you've moved through the most challenging parts of the Pathway to Transformation. For Step 6, it may be tempting but don't assume that you need to take immediate action around your goal. In Step 4 and 5, you probably generated an explosive amount of new ways of thinking and seeing, so a host of prospective next actions likely have opened. Take time to sit with, review, and really feel into your next best move. Explore any other Self-Limiting Beliefs that may arise when you change your goal or direction. You can work this path infinite times until you finally land on where and how you want to move forward.

As you do, just know that even a slight inquiry into SLBs can have the alchemical result you're looking for and you never know when something will flip. Give yourself a pat on the back while you're at it. Exploring Limitations and SLBs isn't necessarily the path of least resistance but it can and does lead to greater freedom.

After all that work, what I'd like to tell you what I know to be true, which is that my life got a lot easier when I made this pathway a life practice. It surprised me more than anyone to discover that one of the most daunting obstacles in my life—my shaky hand—was ultimately accelerated into a more serious problem by me, by my way of seeing and believing. Once I stepped past the fear of inquiring into my beliefs and instead got curious, really curious, the brightest bulb you can imagine switched on.

There is no changing the reality that life will always present us with mountains to climb, oceans to swim, and storms to weather—Limitations we cannot control—but when we learn to let go of, or at least hold less tightly, our ideas about those storms, then so many good things can happen.

Questions
&
Resources

Frequently Asked Questions

Q: I don't vibe with the word "belief" relative to this path. Can you say more about that?

A: Some of you may associate the word 'belief' with faith, or devotion to a spiritual practice or commitment. A belief, in this context, is defined as an attitude, an opinion, an idea, or prop-osition about the world that we hold true with a capital T. This belief may have been unquestioned before, this is normal, be-cause our beliefs are based on varied, personal experiences rather than on objective, absolute truth.

Q: I don't think I'M generating the obstacles in my life. I think they're outside of me.

A: As is the case with Limitations, it is often accurate that the obstacles we run into are, in fact, outside of our doing. If I dream of playing professional basketball but I am only 5'4," indeed, that can be understood as an obstruction to that dream that I have little to no control over. What the Pathway to Transformation is interested in are those obstructions that are perceived rather than actual and can be adapted if we are willing to play with them or hold them differently. It's natural to assume that our personal ideas and concepts about reality are eternally real and would hold up in any environment. But the truth is that many of our notions about life and work are malleable and simply unexamined. These beliefs are actually generated in our own minds rather than delivered to us from any objective meaning in the world.

Q: Is it weird to have self-limiting beliefs? Are there people who don't have any?

A: The short answer: All people have belief systems that are required to navigate being alive. The vast majority of our beliefs are unproblematic, meaning that they do not cause friction with reality and so are harmonious enough to go unnoticed and let us make it through each day. These beliefs only become self-limiting when they conflict with something in our experience and stop the flow of energy, action and relationship.

Q: The concept of SLBs is fascinating. What books or resources would you recommend to further explore self-limiting beliefs?

A:
Mindset, by Carol Dweck
Deviate, by Beau Lotto
The Work, by Byron Katie
The Center for Deep Self Design with Sunni Brown (contributor)
Internal Family Systems, an inner science method by Dr. Richard Schwartz
Thinkertoys, by Michael Michalko
Lateral Thinking, by Edward de Bono

credits and what not:

Through individual work, deep thought, and collaboration this packet was produced by Phil Hansen, Katie Marek, and Sunni Brown.

Special thanks to all those who shared limitations with me and to Sarah who was so eloquent.

I am always delighted to hear your thoughts whether they be suggestions or disagreements with this packet. Your words may lead to future changes and adjustments. If you'd like to reach out please email me at
iam@philinthecircle.com
or leave a Voice Mail at 651-321-4996

To find more about my Art please visit
www.philinthecircle.com

Thankyou!

illustrations by Katie Marek

75785022R00022

Made in the USA
Middletown, DE
07 June 2018